# MEL BAY'S
# Guitar Chords

This book was created in response to many requests for a catalog of elementary guitar chords arranged in a photo-diagram form for maximum ease in understanding and playing.

1 2 3 4 5 6 7 8 9 0

**Barre and rhythm power forms will be found on pages 41 through 48.**

The correct way to hold the guitar.

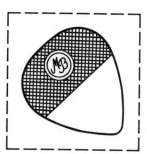

This is the pick.

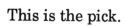

Hold it in this manner firmly between
the thumb and first finger.

⊓ = down stroke of the pick.

## THE LEFT HAND (L.H.)

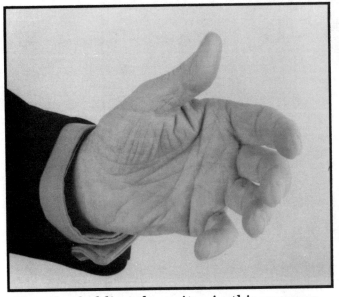

Practice holding the guitar in this manner.

## THE LEFT-HAND POSITION

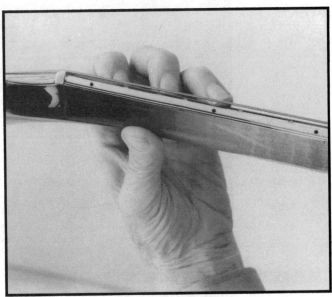

Keep the palm of the hand away from the neck.

X = Do not play string

O = Open string

⊗ = Deaden string

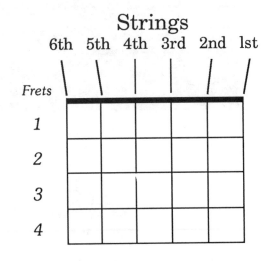

**B₇**

Do Not Play

Open String

Left-Hand Fingering

B D♯ A B F♯

Chordal Notes

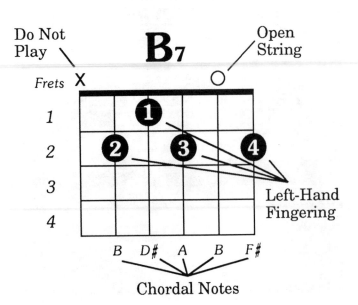

Deadened or Muffled String

Do Not Play

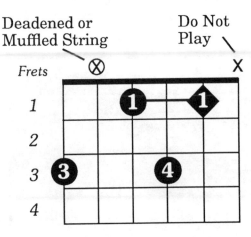

The six open strings of the guitar will be of the same pitch as the six notes shown in the illustration of the piano keyboard. Note that five of the strings are below the middle C of the piano keyboard.

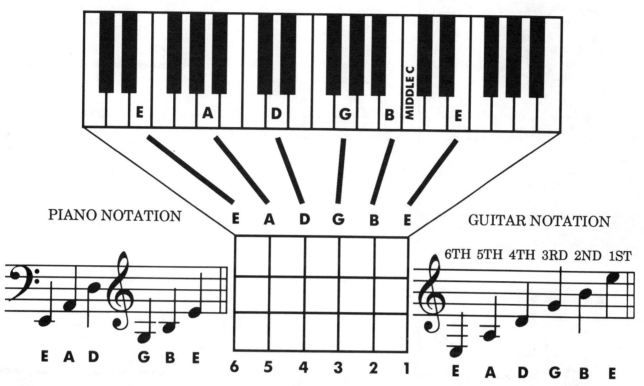

ANOTHER METHOD OF TUNING

1. Tune the 6th string in unison with the **E** or 12th white key to the LEFT of MIDDLE C on the piano.

2. Place the finger behind the fifth fret of the 6th string. This will give you the tone or pitch of the 5th string (**A**).

3. Place finger behind the fifth fret of the 5th string to get the pitch of the 4th string (**D**).

4. Repeat same procedure to obtain the pitch of the 3rd string (**G**).

5. Place finger behind the fourth fret of the 3rd string to get the pitch of the 2nd string (**B**).

6. Place finger behind the fifth fret of the 2nd string to get the pitch of the 1st string (**E**).

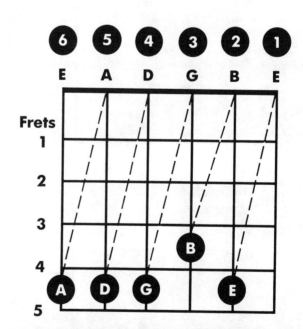

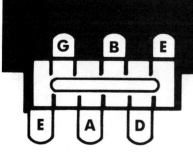

# PITCH PIPES

Pitch pipes with instructions for their usage may be obtained at any music store. Each pipe will have the correct pitch of each guitar string and is recommended to be used when a piano is not available.

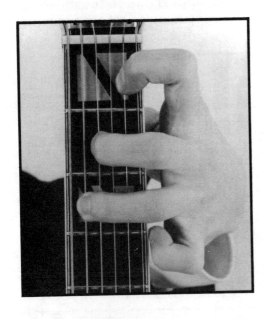

# C

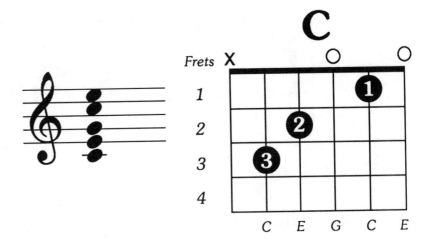

| Frets | X | | | O | | O |
|---|---|---|---|---|---|---|
| 1 | | | | | ① | |
| 2 | | | ② | | | |
| 3 | | ③ | | | | |
| 4 | | | | | | |
| | | C | E | G | C | E |

# F

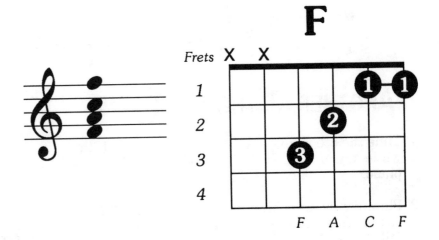

| Frets | X | X | | | | |
|---|---|---|---|---|---|---|
| 1 | | | | | ① | ① |
| 2 | | | | ② | | |
| 3 | | | ③ | | | |
| 4 | | | | | | |
| | | | F | A | C | F |

# G

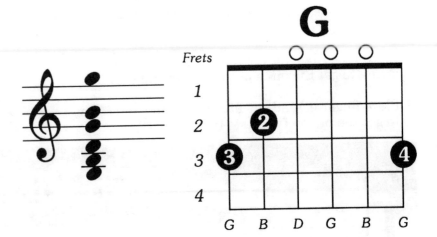

| Frets | | | O | O | O | |
|---|---|---|---|---|---|---|
| 1 | | | | | | |
| 2 | | ② | | | | |
| 3 | ③ | | | | | ④ |
| 4 | | | | | | |
| | G | B | D | G | B | G |

## D

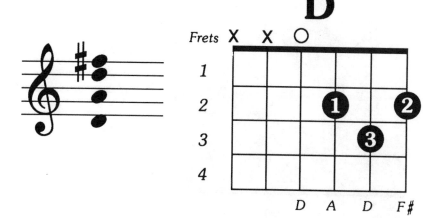

| Frets | X | X | O | | |
|---|---|---|---|---|---|
| 1 | | | | | |
| 2 | | | ① | | ② |
| 3 | | | | ③ | |
| 4 | | | | | |

D   A   D   F#

## A

| Frets | X | O | | | O |
|---|---|---|---|---|---|
| 1 | | | | | |
| 2 | | | ② | ③ | ④ |
| 3 | | | | | |
| 4 | | | | | |

A   E   A   C#   E

## E

| Frets | O | | | O | O |
|---|---|---|---|---|---|
| 1 | | | ① | | |
| 2 | ② | ③ | | | |
| 3 | | | | | |
| 4 | | | | | |

E   B   E   G#   B   E

# B♭

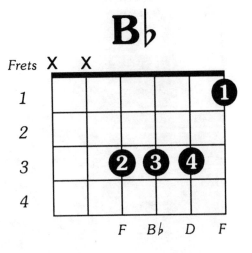

F   B♭   D   F

# E♭

Frets X X

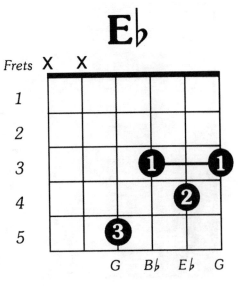

G   B♭   E♭   G

# A♭

Frets X X

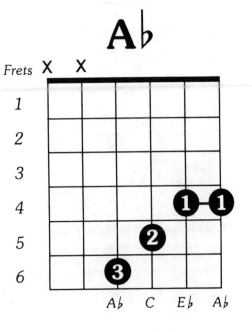

A♭   C   E♭   A♭

# D♭

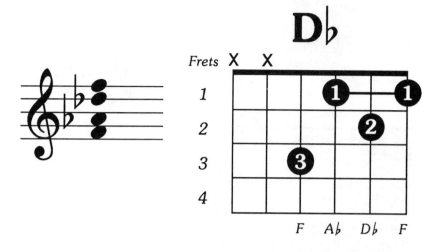

Frets X X

| | | 1 | | 1 |
|---|---|---|---|---|
| | | | 2 | |
| | 3 | | | |
| | | | | |

F  A♭  D♭  F

# G♭ or F#

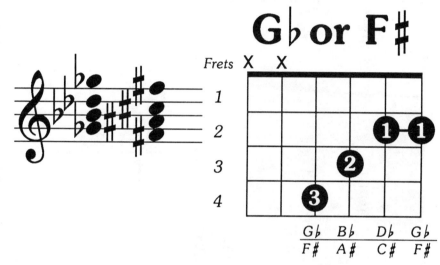

Frets X X

| | | | 1 | 1 |
|---|---|---|---|---|
| | | 2 | | |
| | 3 | | | |

G♭  B♭  D♭  G♭
F#  A#  C#  F#

# B

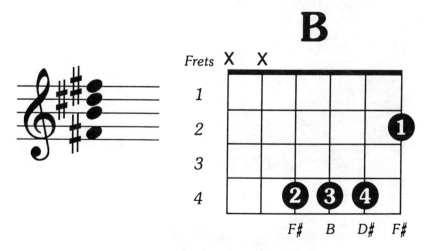

Frets X X

| | | | | 1 |
|---|---|---|---|---|
| | | | | |
| 2 | 3 | 4 | |

F#  B  D#  F#

(m = minor)

## Cm

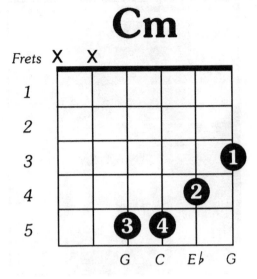

| Frets | X | X | | | |
|---|---|---|---|---|---|
| 1 | | | | | |
| 2 | | | | | |
| 3 | | | | | ① |
| 4 | | | | ② | |
| 5 | | | ③ | ④ | |
| | | | G | C | E♭ G |

## Fm

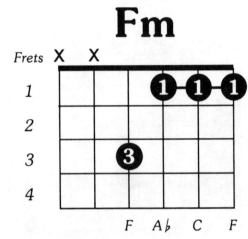

| Frets | X | X | | | |
|---|---|---|---|---|---|
| 1 | | | ① | ① | ① |
| 2 | | | | | |
| 3 | | | ③ | | |
| 4 | | | | | |
| | | | F | A♭ | C F |

## Gm

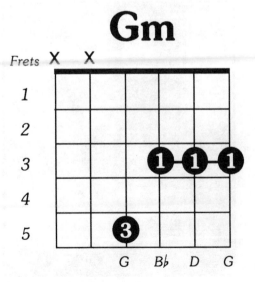

| Frets | X | X | | | |
|---|---|---|---|---|---|
| 1 | | | | | |
| 2 | | | | | |
| 3 | | | ① | ① | ① |
| 4 | | | | | |
| 5 | | | ③ | | |
| | | | G | B♭ | D G |

10

# Dm

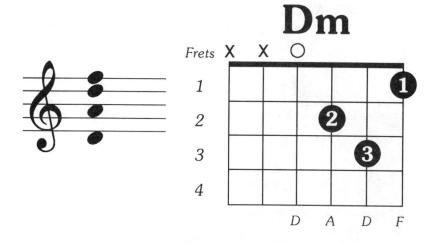

Frets X    X    ◯

| | | | | |
|---|---|---|---|---|
| 1 | | | | ❶ |
| 2 | | | ❷ | |
| 3 | | | | ❸ |
| 4 | | | | |

D    A    D    F

# Am

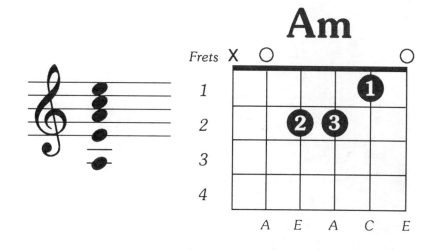

Frets X    ◯          ◯

| | | | | |
|---|---|---|---|---|
| 1 | | | | ❶ |
| 2 | | ❷ | ❸ | |
| 3 | | | | |
| 4 | | | | |

A    E    A    C    E

# Em

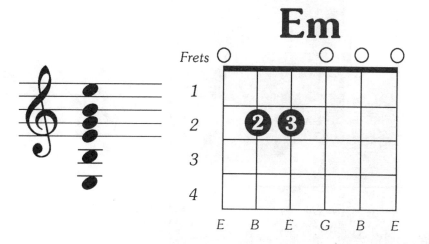

Frets ◯       ◯    ◯    ◯

| | | | | |
|---|---|---|---|---|
| 1 | | | | |
| 2 | ❷ | ❸ | | |
| 3 | | | | |
| 4 | | | | |

E    B    E    G    B    E

# B♭m

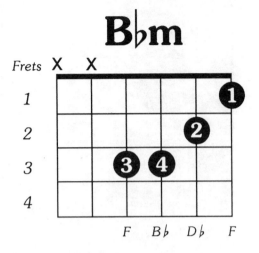

| Frets | X | X | | | | |
|---|---|---|---|---|---|---|
| 1 | | | | | | ➊ |
| 2 | | | | | ➋ | |
| 3 | | | ➌ | ➍ | | |
| 4 | | | | | | |
| | | | F | B♭ | D♭ | F |

# E♭m

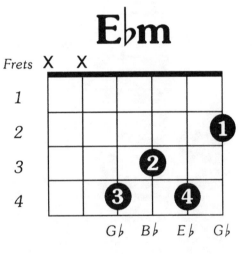

| Frets | X | X | | | | |
|---|---|---|---|---|---|---|
| 1 | | | | | | |
| 2 | | | | | | ➊ |
| 3 | | | | ➋ | | |
| 4 | | | ➌ | | ➍ | |
| | | | G♭ | B♭ | E♭ | G♭ |

# A♭m

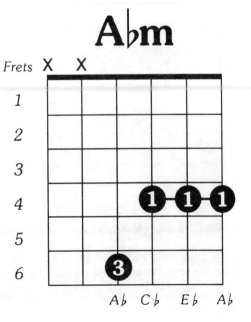

| Frets | X | X | | | | |
|---|---|---|---|---|---|---|
| 1 | | | | | | |
| 2 | | | | | | |
| 3 | | | | | | |
| 4 | | | | ➊ | ➊ | ➊ |
| 5 | | | | | | |
| 6 | | | ➌ | | | |
| | | | A♭ | C♭ | E♭ | A♭ |

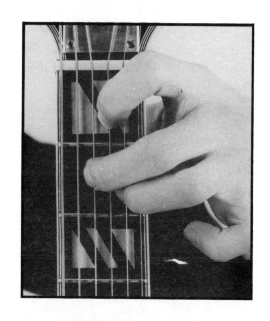

# D♭m

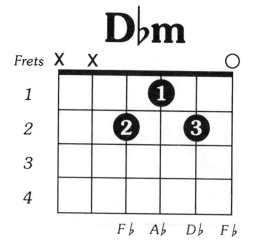

| Frets | X | X | | | O |
|---|---|---|---|---|---|
| 1 | | | | ❶ | |
| 2 | | | ❷ | | ❸ |
| 3 | | | | | |
| 4 | | | | | |

F♭  A♭  D♭  F♭

# G♭m or F♯m

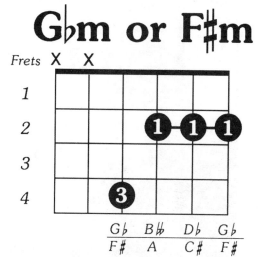

| Frets | X | X | | | |
|---|---|---|---|---|---|
| 1 | | | | | |
| 2 | | | ❶ | ❶ | ❶ |
| 3 | | | | | |
| 4 | | ❸ | | | |

G♭  B♭♭  D♭  G♭
F♯  A  C♯  F♯

# Bm

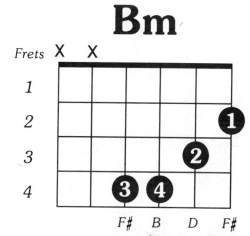

| Frets | X | X | | | |
|---|---|---|---|---|---|
| 1 | | | | | |
| 2 | | | | | ❶ |
| 3 | | | | ❷ | |
| 4 | | | ❸ | ❹ | |

F♯  B  D  F♯

(7 = seventh chord)

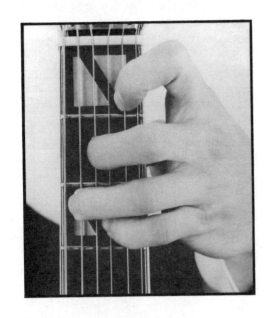

## C₇

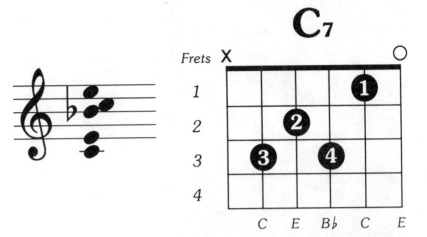

## F₇

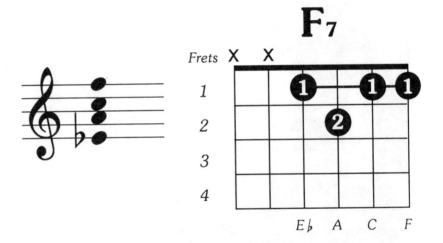

## G₇

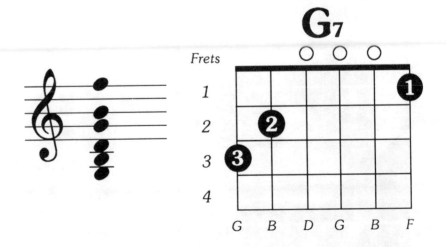

# D₇

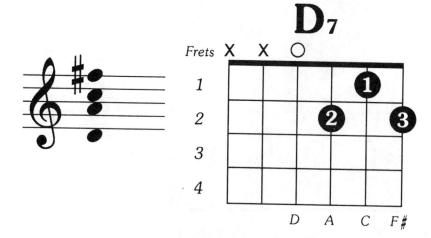

Frets X X O

| | | | 1 | 3 |
|---|---|---|---|---|
| | | | 2 | |
| | | | | |
| | | | | |

D A C F#

# A₇

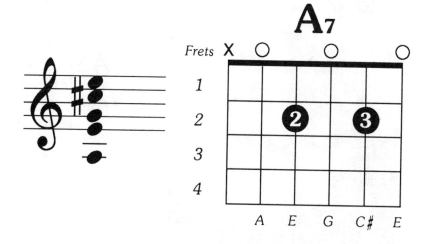

Frets X O O O

| | | 2 | | 3 | |
| D | A | E | G | C# | E |

# E₇

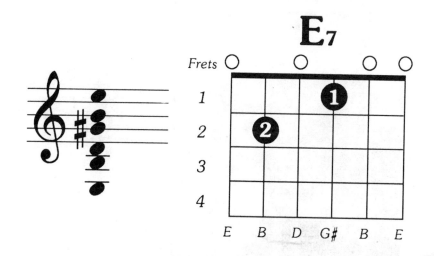

Frets O O O O

| | 2 | | 1 | | |
| E | B | D | G# | B | E |

# B♭7

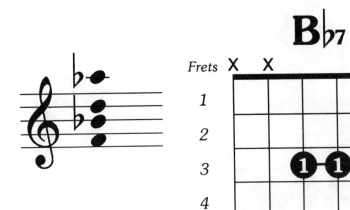

Frets  X  X

| | 1 | 2 | 3 | 4 |
|---|---|---|---|---|
| 1 | | | | |
| 2 | | | | |
| 3 | ① | ① | ① | |
| 4 | | | | ② |

F  B♭  D  A♭

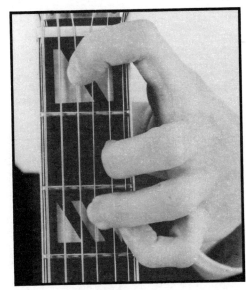

# E♭7

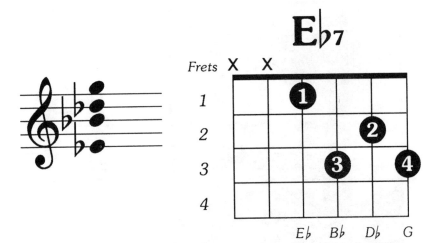

Frets  X  X

| | 1 | 2 | 3 | 4 |
|---|---|---|---|---|
| 1 | | ① | | |
| 2 | | | | ② |
| 3 | | | ③ | ④ |
| 4 | | | | |

E♭  B♭  D♭  G

# A♭7

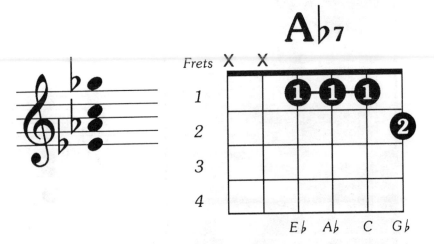

Frets  X  X

| | 1 | 2 | 3 | 4 |
|---|---|---|---|---|
| 1 | | ① | ① | ① |
| 2 | | | | ② |
| 3 | | | | |
| 4 | | | | |

E♭  A♭  C  G♭

## D♭7

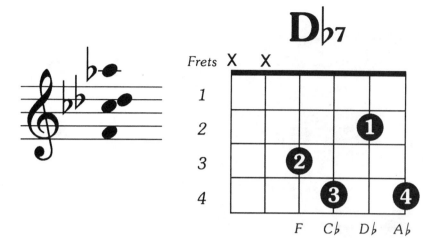

Frets  X  X

| Fret | | | | | |
|---|---|---|---|---|---|
| 1 | | | | | |
| 2 | | | | ❶ | |
| 3 | | ❷ | | | |
| 4 | | | ❸ | | ❹ |

F  C♭  D♭  A♭

## G♭7 or F♯7

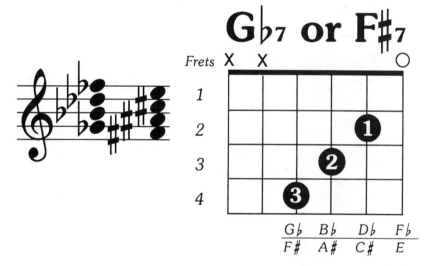

Frets  X  X  ○

| Fret | | | | | |
|---|---|---|---|---|---|
| 1 | | | | | |
| 2 | | | | ❶ | |
| 3 | | | ❷ | | |
| 4 | | ❸ | | | |

G♭  B♭  D♭  F♭
F♯  A♯  C♯  E

## B7

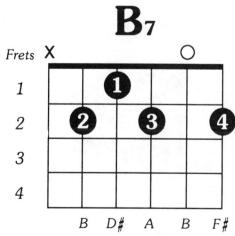

Frets  X  ○

| Fret | | | | | |
|---|---|---|---|---|---|
| 1 | | | ❶ | | |
| 2 | | ❷ | | ❸ | ❹ |
| 3 | | | | | |
| 4 | | | | | |

B  D♯  A  B  F♯

17

Each diminished form can represent four different chords (–, °, or dim = diminished).

# D- Ab- (G#-) B- F-

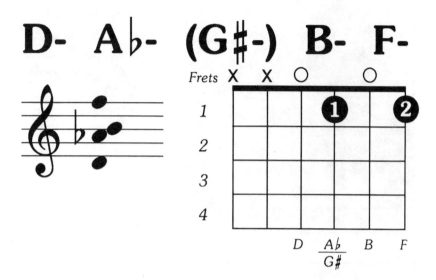

| Frets | X | X | O | | O | |
|---|---|---|---|---|---|---|
| 1 | | | | ❶ | | ❷ |
| 2 | | | | | | |
| 3 | | | | | | |
| 4 | | | | | | |
| | | D | Ab/G# | B | | F |

# Eb- A- C- (F#-) Gb-

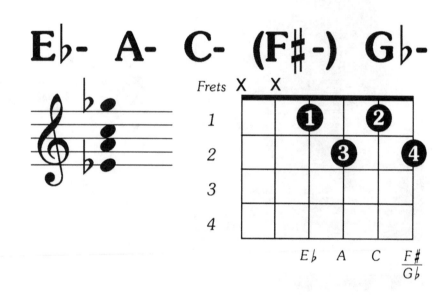

| Frets | X | X | | | | |
|---|---|---|---|---|---|---|
| 1 | | | ❶ | | ❷ | |
| 2 | | | | ❸ | | ❹ |
| 3 | | | | | | |
| 4 | | | | | | |
| | | Eb | A | C | F#/Gb | |

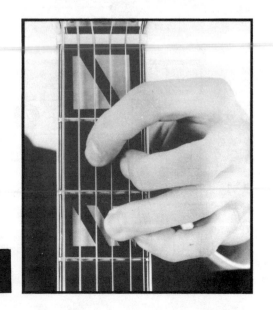

# E- Bb- Db- (C#-) G-

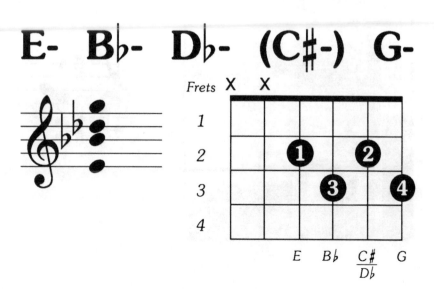

| Frets | X | X | | | | |
|---|---|---|---|---|---|---|
| 1 | | | | | | |
| 2 | | | ❶ | | ❷ | |
| 3 | | | | ❸ | | ❹ |
| 4 | | | | | | |
| | | E | Bb | C#/Db | | G |

# THE AUGMENTED CHORDS

Each form represents three chords (+, aug = augmented).

## E+   A♭+   (G♯+)   C+

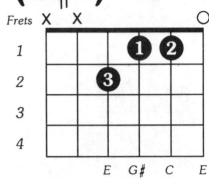

E   G♯   C   E

## F+   A+   (D♭+)   C♯+

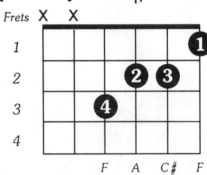

F   A   C♯   F

## (F♯+)   G♭+   B♭+   D+

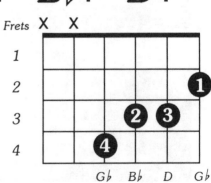

G♭   B♭   D   G♭

## G+   B+   (E♭+)   D♯+

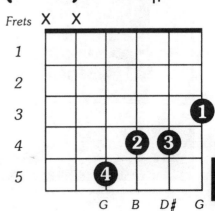

G   B   D♯   G

19

(9 = ninth)

## C₉

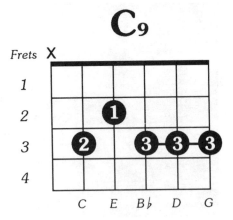

Frets — X

| 1 | | | | | |
| 2 | | | ① | | |
| 3 | ② | | ③ | ③ | ③ |
| 4 | | | | | |

C   E   B♭   D   G

## F₉

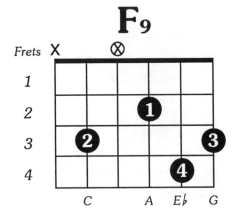

Frets — X      ⊗

| 1 | | | | | |
| 2 | | | | ① | |
| 3 | | ② | | | ③ |
| 4 | | | | ④ | |

C     A   E♭   G

## G₉

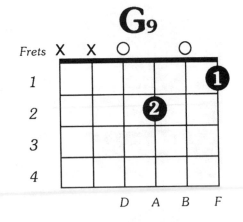

Frets — X  X  ○    ○

| 1 | | | | | ① |
| 2 | | | | ② | |
| 3 | | | | | |
| 4 | | | | | |

D   A   B   F

## D₉

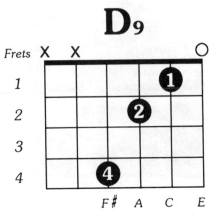

Frets — X  X       ○

| 1 | | | | ① | |
| 2 | | | ② | | |
| 3 | | | | | |
| 4 | | ④ | | | |

F♯  A   C   E

# A₉

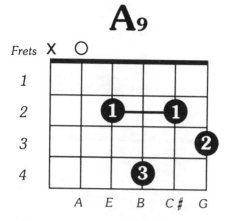

Frets X O

| 1 | | | | | |
| 2 | | ① | | ① | |
| 3 | | | | | ② |
| 4 | | | ③ | | |

A  E  B  C♯  G

# E₉

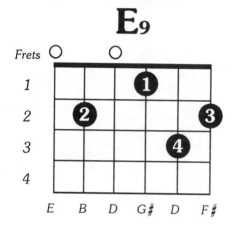

Frets O   O

| 1 | | | ① | | |
| 2 | ② | | | | ③ |
| 3 | | | | ④ | |
| 4 | | | | | |

E  B  D  G♯  D  F♯

# B♭₉

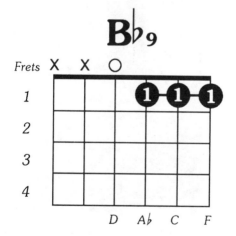

Frets X X O

| 1 | | | | ① | ① | ① |
| 2 | | | | | | |
| 3 | | | | | | |
| 4 | | | | | | |

D  A♭  C  F

# E♭₉

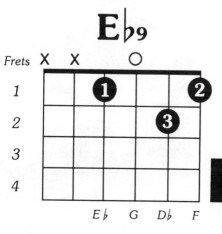

Frets X X   O

| 1 | | | ① | | ② |
| 2 | | | | ③ | |
| 3 | | | | | |
| 4 | | | | | |

E♭  G  D♭  F

21

## A♭9

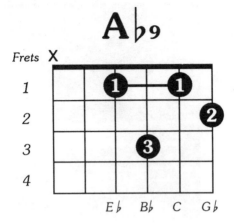

| Frets | X | | | | |
|---|---|---|---|---|---|
| 1 | | | ① | | ① |
| 2 | | | | | ② |
| 3 | | | | ③ | |
| 4 | | | | | |

E♭   B♭   C   G♭

## D♭9

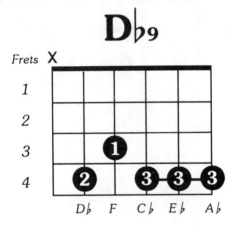

| Frets | X | | | | |
|---|---|---|---|---|---|
| 1 | | | | | |
| 2 | | | | | |
| 3 | | | ① | | |
| 4 | | ② | | ③ ③ ③ | |

D♭   F   C♭   E♭   A♭

## G♭9 or F♯9

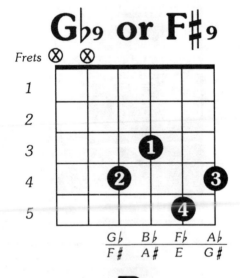

| Frets | ⊗ | ⊗ | | | |
|---|---|---|---|---|---|
| 1 | | | | | |
| 2 | | | | | |
| 3 | | | | ① | |
| 4 | | | ② | | ③ |
| 5 | | | | ④ | |

G♭   B♭   F♭   A♭
F♯   A♯   E   G♯

## B9

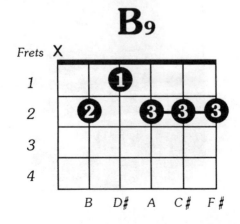

| Frets | X | | | | |
|---|---|---|---|---|---|
| 1 | | | ① | | |
| 2 | | ② | | ③ ③ ③ | |
| 3 | | | | | |
| 4 | | | | | |

B   D♯   A   C♯   F♯

(ma7, ⁷ = major seventh)

### C ma7

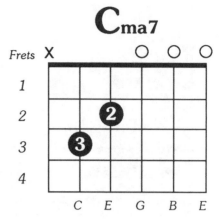

Frets
X    ○  ○  ○
1
2
3
4

C  E  G  B  E

### F ma7

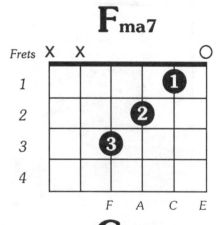

Frets
X  X        ○
1
2
3
4

F  A  C  E

### G ma7

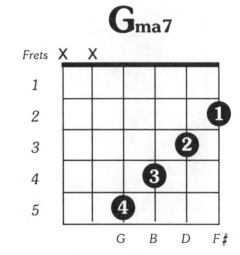

Frets
X  X
1
2
3
4
5

G  B  D  F#

### D ma7

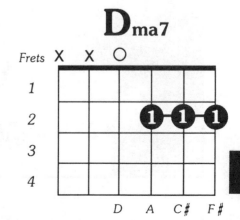

Frets
X  X  ○
1
2
3
4

D  A  C#  F#

23

## A<sub>ma7</sub>

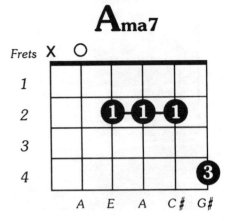

Frets X ○

A E A C♯ G♯

## E<sub>ma7</sub>

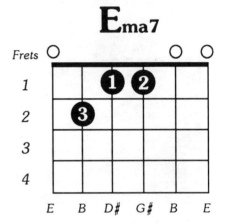

Frets ○ ○ ○

E B D♯ G♯ B E

## B♭<sub>ma7</sub>

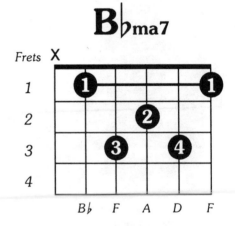

Frets X

B♭ F A D F

24

## E♭<sub>ma7</sub>

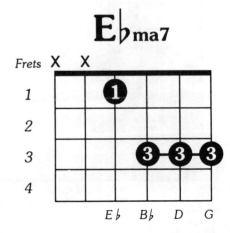

Frets X X

E♭ B♭ D G

## A♭ma7

## D♭ma7

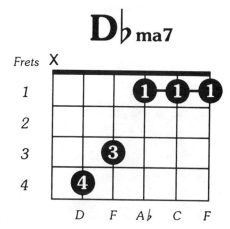

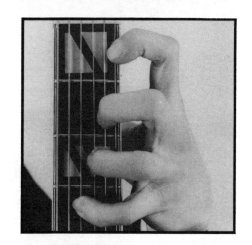

## G♭ma7 or F♯ma7

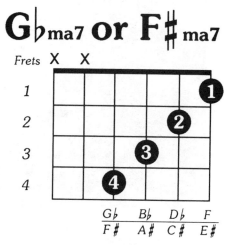

## Bma7

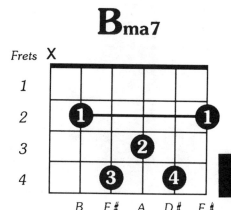

25

(m7 = minor seventh)

## Cm7

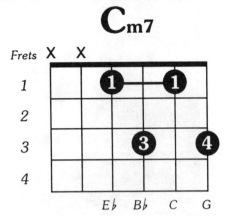

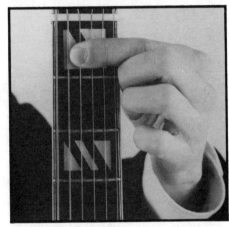

## Fm7

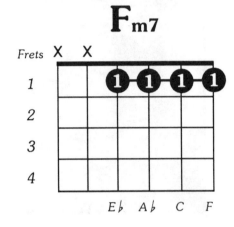

## Gm7

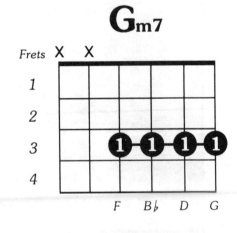

## Dm7

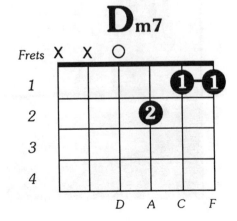

26

## A<sub>m7</sub>

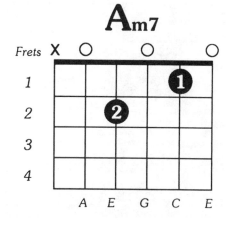

Frets — X O O O
A E G C E

## E<sub>m7</sub>

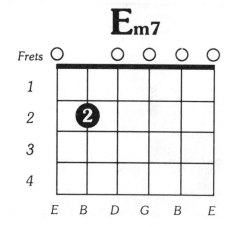

Frets — O O O O
E B D G B E

## B♭<sub>m7</sub>

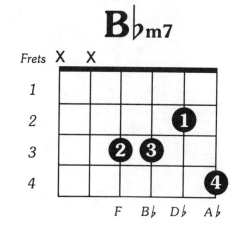

Frets — X X
F B♭ D♭ A♭

## E♭<sub>m7</sub>

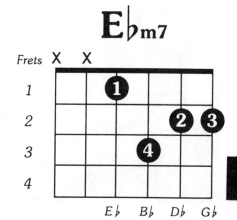

Frets — X X
E♭ B♭ D♭ G♭

27

## A♭m7

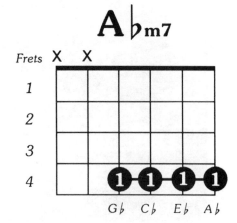

| Frets | X | X | | | |
|---|---|---|---|---|---|
| 1 | | | | | |
| 2 | | | | | |
| 3 | | | | | |
| 4 | | ① | ① | ① | ① |

G♭  C♭  E♭  A♭

## D♭m7

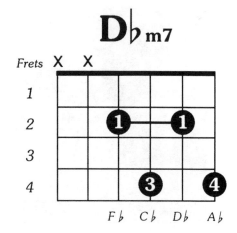

| Frets | X | X | | | |
|---|---|---|---|---|---|
| 1 | | | | | |
| 2 | | ① | | ① | |
| 3 | | | | | |
| 4 | | | ③ | | ④ |

F♭  C♭  D♭  A♭

## G♭m7 or F♯m7

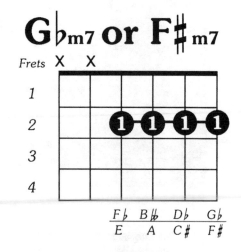

| Frets | X | X | | | |
|---|---|---|---|---|---|
| 1 | | | | | |
| 2 | | ① | ① | ① | ① |
| 3 | | | | | |
| 4 | | | | | |

F♭  B♭♭  D♭  G♭
E    A    C♯   F♯

## Bm7

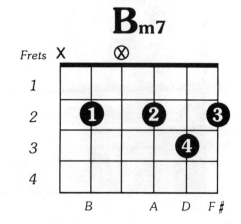

| Frets | X | | ⊗ | | |
|---|---|---|---|---|---|
| 1 | | | | | |
| 2 | | ① | | ② | ③ |
| 3 | | | | ④ | |
| 4 | | | | | |

B    A    D    F♯

28

(7+5 = seventh augmented fifth)

## C₇₊₅

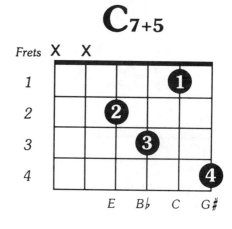

Frets X X
1
2
3
4

E    B♭    C    G♯

## F₇₊₅

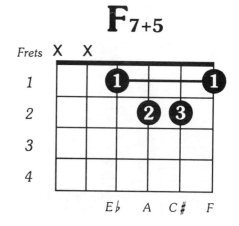

Frets X X
1
2
3
4

E♭    A    C♯    F

## G₇₊₅

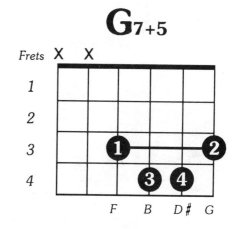

Frets X X
1
2
3
4

F    B    D♯    G

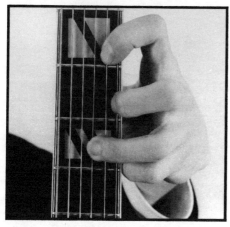

## D₇₊₅

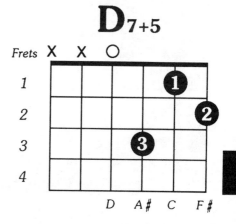

Frets X X O
1
2
3
4

D    A♯    C    F♯

29

# THE SEVENTH AUGMENTED FIFTH

## A7+5

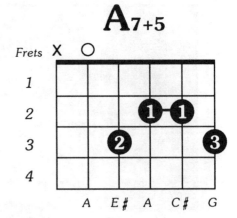

| Frets | X | O | | | |
|---|---|---|---|---|---|
| 1 | | | | | |
| 2 | | | | ① | ① |
| 3 | | ② | | | ③ |
| 4 | | | | | |

A  E♯  A  C♯  G

## E7+5

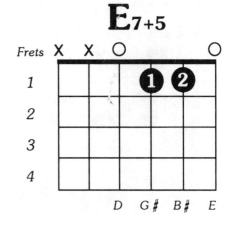

| Frets | X | X | O | | O |
|---|---|---|---|---|---|
| 1 | | | | ① | ② |
| 2 | | | | | |
| 3 | | | | | |
| 4 | | | | | |

D  G♯  B♯  E

## B♭7+5

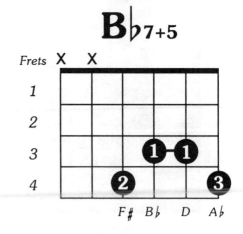

| Frets | X | X | | | |
|---|---|---|---|---|---|
| 1 | | | | | |
| 2 | | | | | |
| 3 | | | | ① | ① |
| 4 | | ② | | | ③ |

F♯  B♭  D  A♭

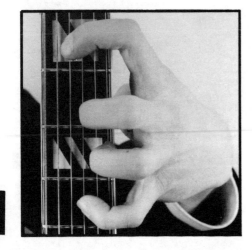

## E♭7+5

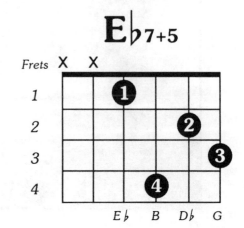

| Frets | X | X | | | |
|---|---|---|---|---|---|
| 1 | | ① | | | |
| 2 | | | | ② | |
| 3 | | | | | ③ |
| 4 | | | ④ | | |

E♭  B  D♭  G

## A♭7+5

| Frets | X | X | | | |
|---|---|---|---|---|---|
| 1 | | | | ①—① | |
| 2 | | | ② | | ③ |
| 3 | | | | | |
| 4 | | | | | |

E   A♭   C   G♭

## D♭7+5

| Frets | X | X | | | |
|---|---|---|---|---|---|
| 1 | | | | | |
| 2 | | | | | ① |
| 3 | | | ② | | |
| 4 | | | | ③ | |
| 5 | | | | | ④ |

F   C♭   D♭   A

## G♭7+5 or F♯7+5

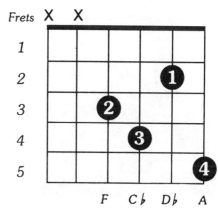

| Frets | X | X | | | |
|---|---|---|---|---|---|
| 1 | | | | | |
| 2 | | | ①— | —————① | |
| 3 | | | | ② | ③ |
| 4 | | | | | |

F♭   B♭   D   G♭
E   A♯   C𝄪   F♯

## B7+5

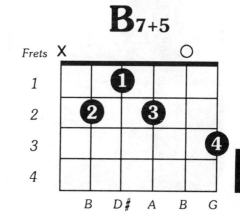

| Frets | X | | | O | |
|---|---|---|---|---|---|
| 1 | | | ① | | |
| 2 | | ② | | ③ | |
| 3 | | | | | ④ |
| 4 | | | | | |

B   D♯   A   B   G

**31**

(7-5 = seventh diminished fifth)

## C<sub>7-5</sub>

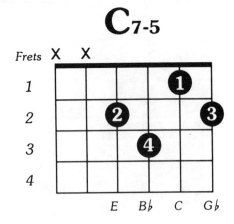

*Frets*  X  X

|   | E | Bb | C | Gb |

## F<sub>7-5</sub>

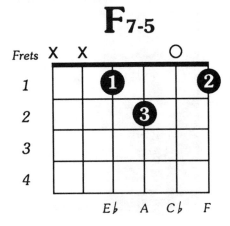

*Frets*  X  X        O

|   | Eb | A | Cb | F |

## G<sub>7-5</sub>

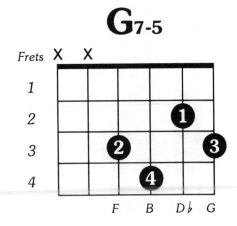

*Frets*  X  X

|   | F | B | Db | G |

## D<sub>7-5</sub>

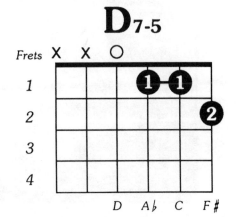

*Frets*  X  X  O

|   | D | Ab | C | F# |

## A₇₋₅

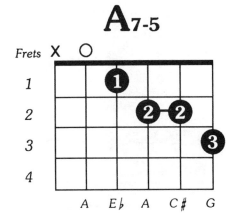

Frets: X  O

| | A | Eb | A | C# | G |

## E₇₋₅

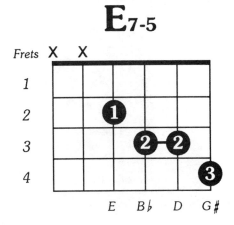

Frets: X  X

| E | Bb | D | G# |

## Bb₇₋₅

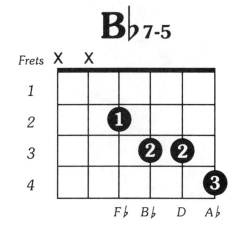

Frets: X  X

| Fb | Bb | D | Ab |

## Eb₇₋₅

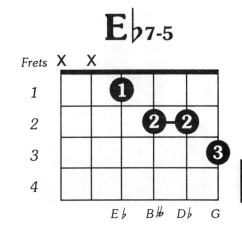

Frets: X  X

| Eb | Bbb | Db | G |

**33**

# THE SEVENTH DIMINISHED FIFTH

### A♭7-5

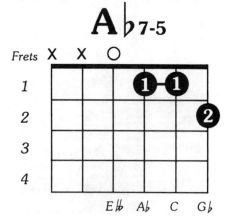

| Frets | X | X | O | | |
|---|---|---|---|---|---|
| 1 | | | ① | ① | |
| 2 | | | | | ② |
| 3 | | | | | |
| 4 | | | | | |

E♭♭  A♭  C  G♭

### D♭7-5

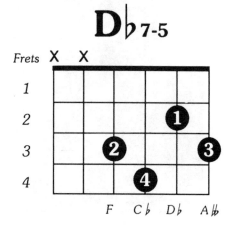

| Frets | X | X | | | |
|---|---|---|---|---|---|
| 1 | | | | | |
| 2 | | | | ① | |
| 3 | | | ② | | ③ |
| 4 | | | | ④ | |

F  C♭  D♭  A♭♭

### G♭7-5 or F♯7-5

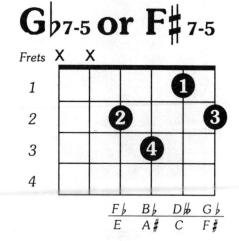

| Frets | X | X | | | |
|---|---|---|---|---|---|
| 1 | | | | ① | |
| 2 | | | ② | | ③ |
| 3 | | | | ④ | |
| 4 | | | | | |

F♭  B♭  D♭♭  G♭
E   A♯  C    F♯

### B7-5

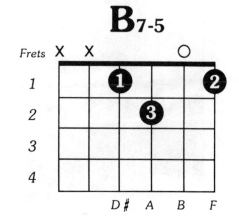

| Frets | X | X | | O | |
|---|---|---|---|---|---|
| 1 | | | ① | | ② |
| 2 | | | | ③ | |
| 3 | | | | | |
| 4 | | | | | |

D♯  A  B  F

34

(6 = sixth)

## C6

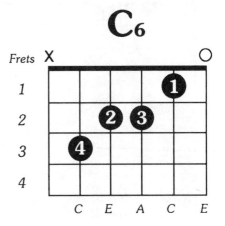

Frets ✕         ◯

1       ①

2    ② ③

3 ④

4

C   E   A   C   E

## F6

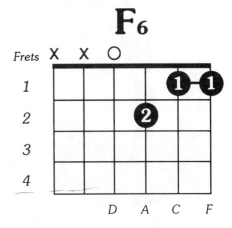

Frets ✕   ✕   ◯

1        ① ①

2      ②

3

4

D   A   C   F

## G6

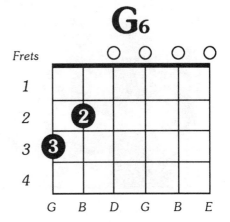

Frets      ◯   ◯   ◯   ◯

1

2   ②

3 ③

4

G   B   D   G   B   E

## D6

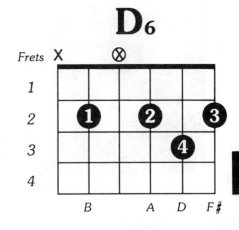

Frets ✕      ⊗

1

2   ①    ②    ③

3       ④

4

B     A   D   F♯

35

## A₆

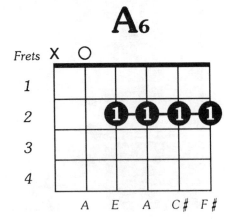

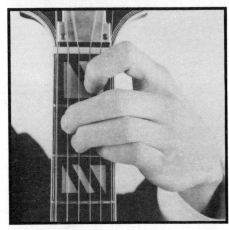

## E₆

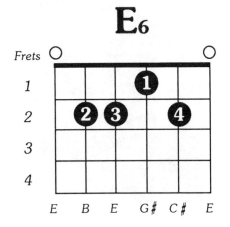

May be omitted
if difficult

## B♭₆

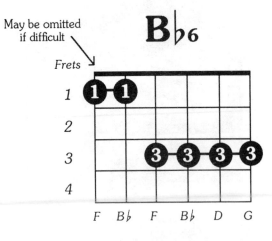

## E♭₆

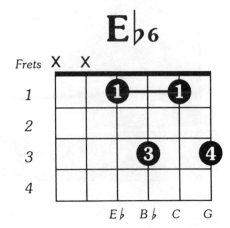

# A♭6

| | | | | | |
|---|---|---|---|---|---|
| 1 | | | ① | ① | ① ① |

E♭   A♭   C   F

# D♭6

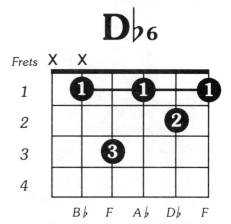

Frets   X   X

B♭   F   A♭   D♭   F

# G♭6 or F♯6

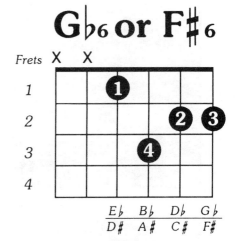

Frets   X   X

$\frac{E♭}{D♯}$   $\frac{B♭}{A♯}$   $\frac{D♭}{C♯}$   $\frac{G♭}{F♯}$

# B6

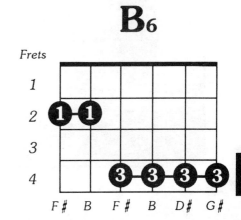

Frets

F♯   B   F♯   B   D♯   G♯

(m6 = minor sixth)

## C<sub>m6</sub>

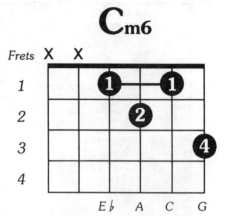

## F<sub>m6</sub>

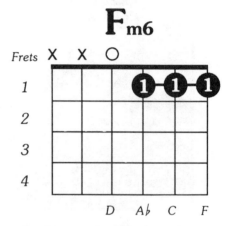

## G<sub>m6</sub>

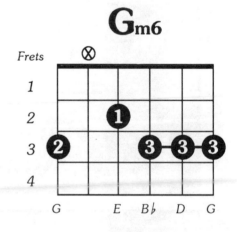

## D<sub>m6</sub>

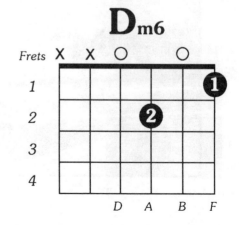

## A<sub>m6</sub>

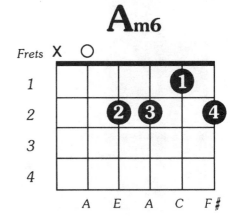

## E<sub>m6</sub>

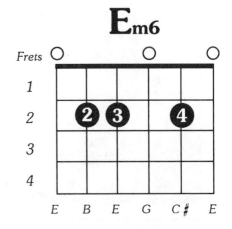

## B♭<sub>m6</sub>

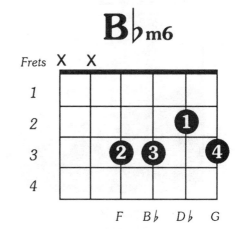

## E♭<sub>m6</sub>

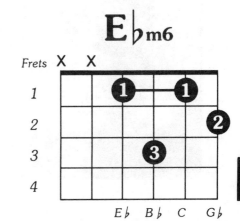

39

## A♭m6

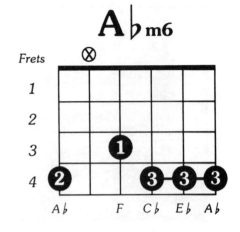

| Frets | ⊗ | | | | |
|---|---|---|---|---|---|
| 1 | | | | | |
| 2 | | | | | |
| 3 | | | ① | | |
| 4 | ② | | | ③ | ③ | ③ |

A♭    F    C♭   E♭   A♭

## D♭m6

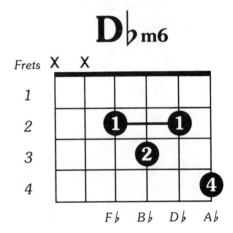

| Frets | X | X | | | |
|---|---|---|---|---|---|
| 1 | | | | | |
| 2 | | | ① | | ① |
| 3 | | | | ② | |
| 4 | | | | | ④ |

F♭   B♭   D♭   A♭

## G♭m6 or F♯m6

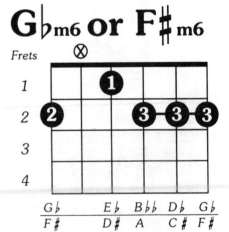

| Frets | ⊗ | | | | |
|---|---|---|---|---|---|
| 1 | | ① | | | |
| 2 | ② | | | ③ | ③ | ③ |
| 3 | | | | | |
| 4 | | | | | |

G♭        E♭   B♭♭  D♭   G♭
F♯        D♯   A    C♯   F♯

## Bm6

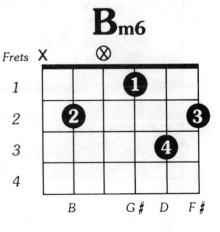

| Frets | X | | ⊗ | | |
|---|---|---|---|---|---|
| 1 | | | | ① | |
| 2 | | ② | | | ③ |
| 3 | | | | ④ | |
| 4 | | | | | |

B        G♯   D    F♯

Note: Each form must be thoroughly mastered before proceeding to the next.

# THE MAJOR CHORDS

⊗ = deaden string. This is done by allowing the unused part of the left hand to touch the strings just enough to kill their sound.

| Frets | 1 | 2 | 3 | 4 | 5 | 6 | 7 | 8 | 9 | 10 |
|---|---|---|---|---|---|---|---|---|---|---|
| Chords | F | F♯ or G♭ | G | A♭ | A | B♭ | B | C | C♯ or D♭ | D |

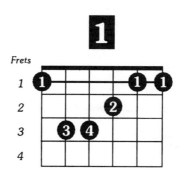

| Frets | 1 | 2 | 3 | 4 | 5 | 6 | 7 | 8 | 9 | 10 |
|---|---|---|---|---|---|---|---|---|---|---|
| Chords | C♯ or D♭ | D | E♭ | E | F | F♯ or G♭ | G | A♭ | A | B♭ |

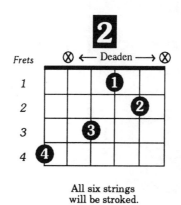

All six strings will be stroked.

| Frets | 1 | 2 | 3 | 4 | 5 | 6 | 7 | 8 | 9 | 10 |
|---|---|---|---|---|---|---|---|---|---|---|
| Chords | A♭ | A | B♭ | B | C | D♭ or C♯ | D | E♭ | E | F |

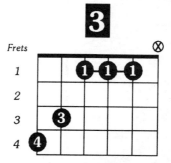

The first string is deadened. Note that the second finger is not used.

# THE MOVABLE RHYTHM CHORDS

## THE MINOR CHORDS

| Frets | 1 | 2 | 3 | 4 | 5 | 6 | 7 | 8 |
|---|---|---|---|---|---|---|---|---|
| Chords | Fm | F♯m or G♭m | Gm | A♭m or G♯m | Am | B♭m | Bm | Cm |

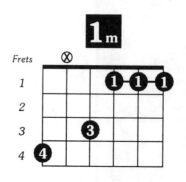

The fifth string is deadened.

| Frets | 1 | 2 | 3 | 4 | 5 | 6 | 7 | 8 |
|---|---|---|---|---|---|---|---|---|
| Chords | Dm | E♭m or D♯m | Em | Fm | G♭m or F♯m | Gm | A♭m or G♯m | Am |

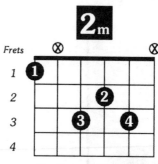

The first and fifth strings
are deadened.

| Frets | 1 | 2 | 3 | 4 | 5 | 6 | 7 | 8 |
|---|---|---|---|---|---|---|---|---|
| Chords | B♭m | Bm | Cm | D♭m or C♯m | Dm | E♭m or D♯m | Em | Fm |

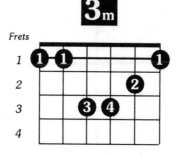

Play each chord chromatically up the fingerboard from the first to the tenth frets. (For a complete detailed study and development of these chords and their progressions, see the *Rhythm Guitar Chord System.*)

## CHORDS DERIVED FROM FORM I⁷

For convenience we use C7 as an example.

### C7

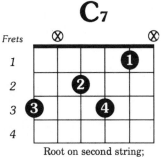

Root on second string; third on fourth string; fifth on sixth string; seventh on third string.

### Cm7

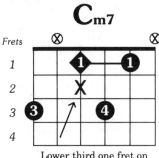

Lower third one fret on fourth string.

### C7sus4

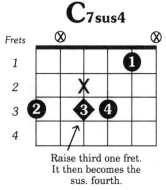

Raise third one fret. It then becomes the sus. fourth.

### C7-5

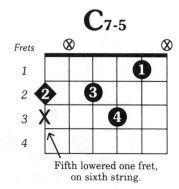

Fifth lowered one fret, on sixth string.

### C7+5

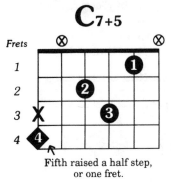

Fifth raised a half step, or one fret.

### Cm7-5

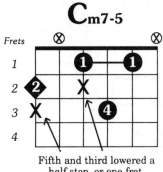

Fifth and third lowered a half step, or one fret.

### C6

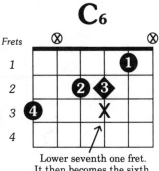

Lower seventh one fret. It then becomes the sixth.

### Cm6

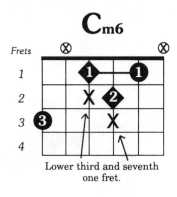

Lower third and seventh one fret.

### C-

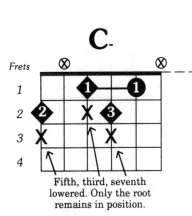

Fifth, third, seventh lowered. Only the root remains in position.

*Derived from C dim.*

### C-add9

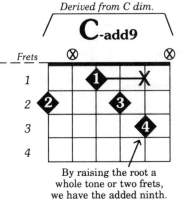

By raising the root a whole tone or two frets, we have the added ninth.

### C9

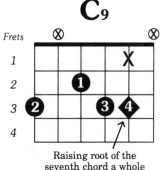

Raising root of the seventh chord a whole tone, or two frets, produces the ninth tone.

### Cm9

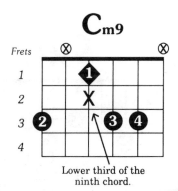

Lower third of the ninth chord.

## C9-5

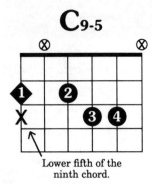

Lower fifth of the
ninth chord.

## C9+5

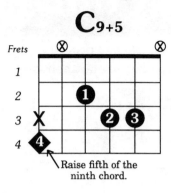

Raise fifth of the
ninth chord.

## Cm9-5

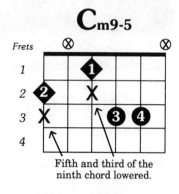

Fifth and third of the
ninth chord lowered.

## C-9

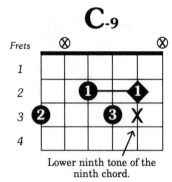

Lower ninth tone of the
ninth chord.

## C-9+5

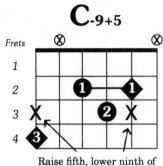

Raise fifth, lower ninth of
the ninth chord.

## C11

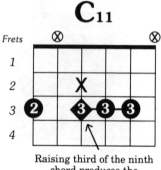

Raising third of the ninth
chord produces the
11th tone.

## C11+

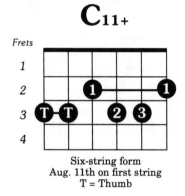

Six-string form
Aug. 11th on first string
T = Thumb

## C⁹/6

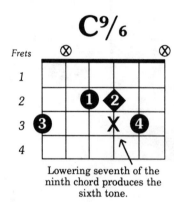

Lowering seventh of the
ninth chord produces the
sixth tone.

## Cm⁹/6

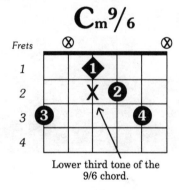

Lower third tone of the
9/6 chord.

## C⁹/6

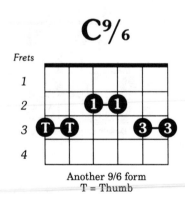

Another 9/6 form
T = Thumb

## C13

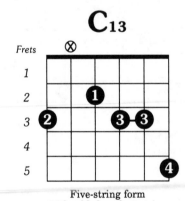

Five-string form
13th added on first string

## C13sus11

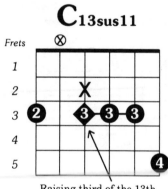

Raising third of the 13th
chord produces the sus.
11th tone.

## C13-9

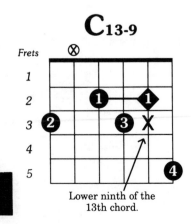

Lower ninth of the
13th chord.

## C13-9

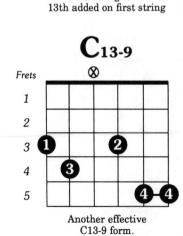

Another effective
C13-9 form.

## C13 ₋₅⁻⁹

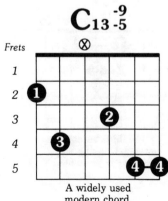

A widely used
modern chord.

# THE MODERN RHYTHM CHORDS

## CHORDS DERIVED FROM FORM III⁷

For convenience we use A7 as an example.

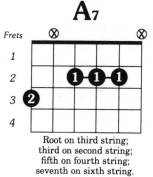

**A₇**

Root on third string;
third on second string;
fifth on fourth string;
seventh on sixth string.

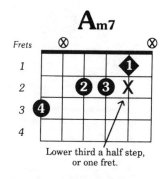

**Aₘ7**

Lower third a half step,
or one fret.

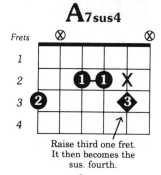

**A₇sus4**

Raise third one fret.
It then becomes the
sus. fourth.

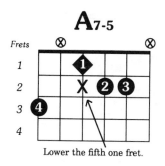

**A₇₋₅**

Lower the fifth one fret.

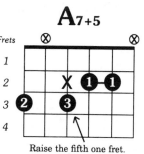

**A₇₊₅**

Raise the fifth one fret.

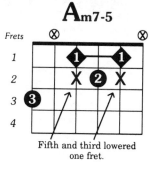

**Aₘ7₋5**

Fifth and third lowered
one fret.

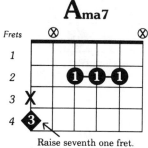

**Aₘₐ7**

Raise seventh one fret.

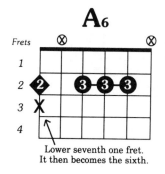

**A₆**

Lower seventh one fret.
It then becomes the sixth.

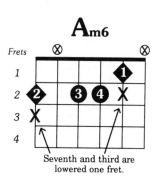

**Aₘ6**

Seventh and third are
lowered one fret.

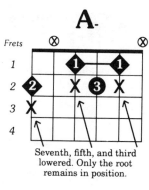

**A₋**

Seventh, fifth, and third
lowered. Only the root
remains in position.

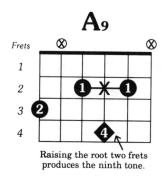

**A₉**

Raising the root two frets
produces the ninth tone.

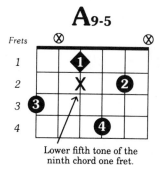

**A₉₋₅**

Lower fifth tone of the
ninth chord one fret.

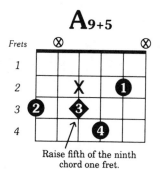

**A₉₊₅**

Raise fifth of the ninth
chord one fret.

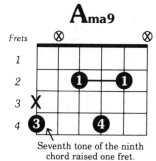

**Aₘₐ9**

Seventh tone of the ninth
chord raised one fret.

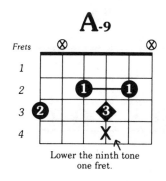

**A₋9**

Lower the ninth tone
one fret.

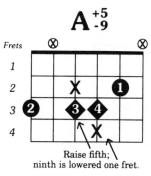

**A$^{+5}_{-9}$**

Raise fifth;
ninth is lowered one fret.

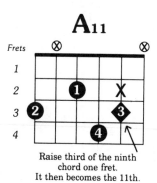

**A₁₁**

Raise third of the ninth
chord one fret.
It then becomes the 11th.

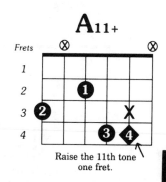

**A₁₁₊**

Raise the 11th tone
one fret.

45

# CHORDS DERIVED FROM FORM V⁷

For convenience we use G7 as an example.

## G₇

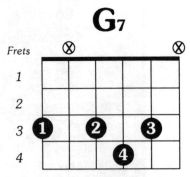

Root on sixth string;
third on third string;
fifth on second string;
seventh on fourth string.

## Gₘ₇

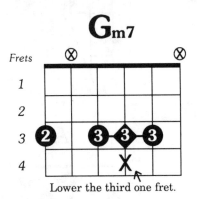

Lower the third one fret.

## G₇sus4

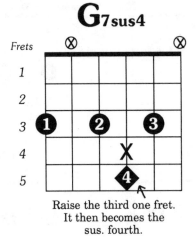

Raise the third one fret.
It then becomes the
sus. fourth.

## G₇₋₅

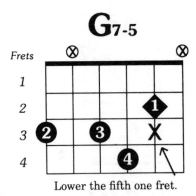

Lower the fifth one fret.

## G₇₊₅

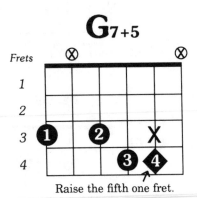

Raise the fifth one fret.

## Gₘ₇₋₅

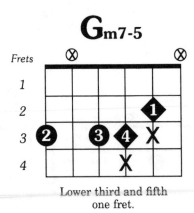

Lower third and fifth
one fret.

## Gₘₐ₇

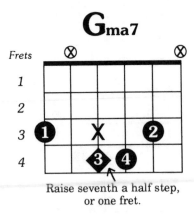

Raise seventh a half step,
or one fret.

## G₆

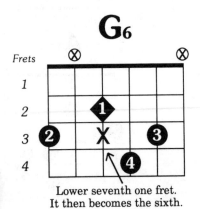

Lower seventh one fret.
It then becomes the sixth.

## Gₘ₆

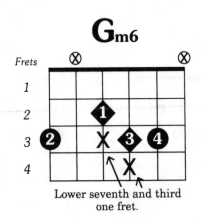

Lower seventh and third
one fret.

## G-

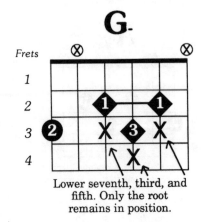

Lower seventh, third, and
fifth. Only the root
remains in position.

# CHORDS DERIVED FROM FORM V⁷

For convenience we use G7 as an example (continued from previous page).

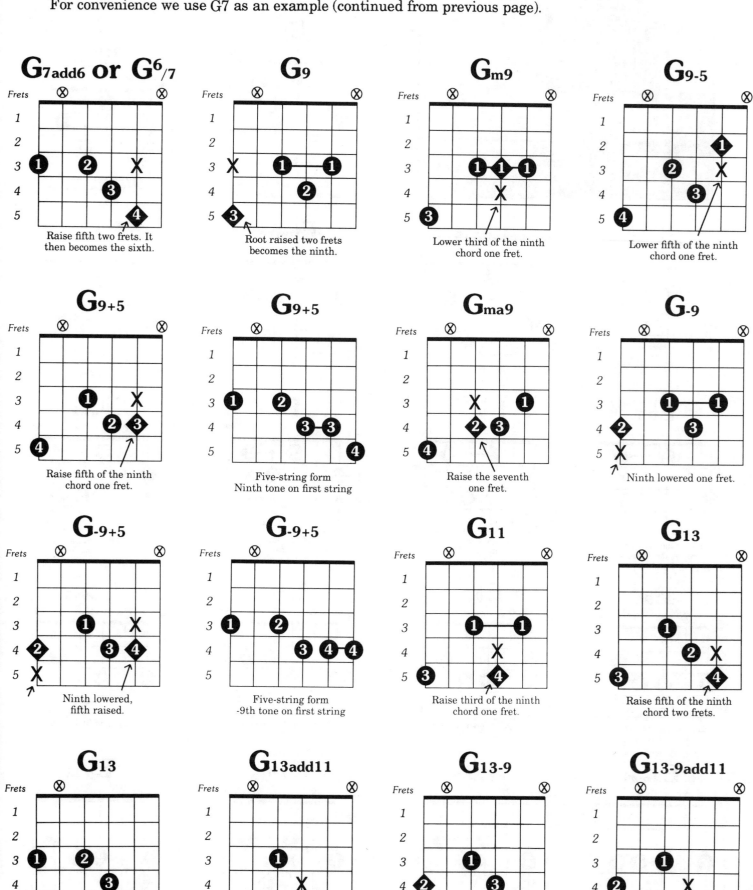

**G7add6 or G6/7** — Raise fifth two frets. It then becomes the sixth.

**G9** — Root raised two frets becomes the ninth.

**Gm9** — Lower third of the ninth chord one fret.

**G9-5** — Lower fifth of the ninth chord one fret.

**G9+5** — Raise fifth of the ninth chord one fret.

**G9+5** — Five-string form Ninth tone on first string

**Gma9** — Raise the seventh one fret.

**G-9** — Ninth lowered one fret.

**G-9+5** — Ninth lowered, fifth raised.

**G-9+5** — Five-string form -9th tone on first string

**G11** — Raise third of the ninth chord one fret.

**G13** — Raise fifth of the ninth chord two frets.

**G13** — Another 13th form

**G13add11** — Raise the third.

**G13-9** — Ninth lowered.

**G13-9add11** — Raise third one fret.

# CHORDS DERIVED FROM FORM VII⁷

For convenience we use E♭7 as an example.

### E♭7
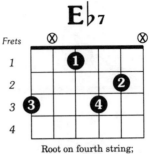

Root on fourth string;
third on sixth string;
fifth on third string;
seventh on second string.

### E♭m7
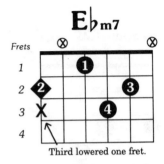

Third lowered one fret.

### E♭7-5
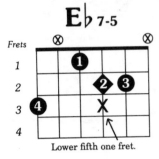

Lower fifth one fret.

### E♭7+5
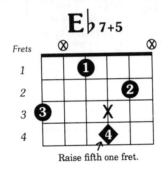

Raise fifth one fret.

### E♭m7-5
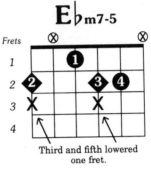

Third and fifth lowered
one fret.

### E♭ma7
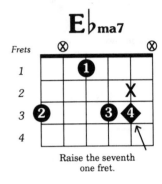

Raise the seventh
one fret.

### E♭6
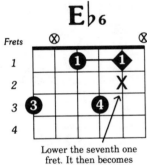

Lower the seventh one
fret. It then becomes
the sixth.

### E♭m6
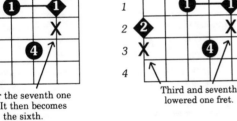

Third and seventh
lowered one fret.

### E♭-
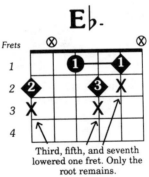

Third, fifth, and seventh
lowered one fret. Only the
root remains.

### E♭ma7♭3
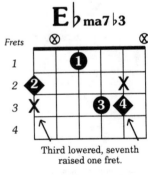

Third lowered, seventh
raised one fret.

### E♭9
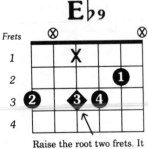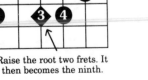

Raise the root two frets. It
then becomes the ninth.

### E♭m9
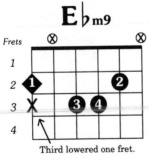

Third lowered one fret.

### E♭9-5
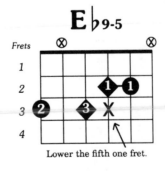

Lower the fifth one fret.

### E♭9+5
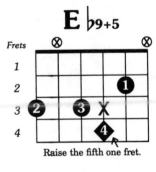

Raise the fifth one fret.

### E♭ma9
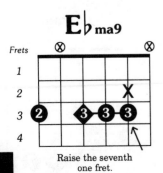

Raise the seventh
one fret.

### E♭-9
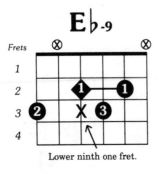

Lower ninth one fret.

### E♭-9+5
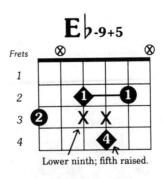

Lower ninth; fifth raised.

### E♭11
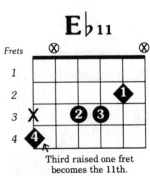

Third raised one fret
becomes the 11th.

48